SALT

Wick Poetry Chapbook Series Four
Maggie Anderson, Editor

How to Paint the Savior Dead
Jason Gray

The Space Between Stars
Matt McBride

Spotlit Girl
Kevin Oberlin

Tornado
Ted Lardner

Song of the Rest of Us
Mindi Kirchner

Salt
Liz Tilton

SALT

Poems by Liz Tilton

The Kent State University Press
Kent, Ohio

© 2009 by Liz Tilton

All rights reserved

Library of Congress Catalog Card Number 2008049183

ISBN 978-1-60635-014 0

Manufactured in the United States of America

The Wick Poetry Series is sponsored in part by the Wick Poetry Center at Kent State University.

Library of Congress Cataloging-in-Publication Data

Tilton, Liz, 1958–

    Salt : poems / by Liz Tilton.

        p.   cm. — (Wick poetry chapbook seires four ; 6)

    ISBN 978-1-60635-014-0 (pbk. : alk. paper) ∞

    I. Title.

    PS 3620.I52S25 2009

    811'.6—dc22   2008049183

British Library Cataloging-in-Publication data are available.

For Deb Fritz

CONTENTS

ACKNOWLEDGMENTS

Thanks to my family: Deb Fritz; Bonnie and Lawrence Tilton; Cameron, Courtney, and Grayson Tilton, and Zane Wilson. Thanks to those who offered encouraging words in hallways, in emails, and in margins of poems and who may be surprised to find themselves listed here: Michael Dumanis, Julianna Gray, Ariana Sophia Kartsonis, Cate Marvin, Nicola Mason, and Will Toedtman. Thanks to faculty at the University of Cincinnati's English department, especially Michael Atkinson, Stan Corkin, John Drury, Russel Durst, Wayne Hall, Jon Kamholtz, Lee Person, Jim Schiff, Lucy Schultz. A very special thanks to Don Bogen for goading the poet, the poems, and the book; and finally thanks to Maggie Anderson for choosing *Salt* and then for shaping it into a better collection.

Grateful acknowledgment is due to the following publications in which a version of these poems previously appeared:
Southern Humanities Review: "Bulldogging, 1924"
Southern Review: "When the Movers Took the Bed"
Valparaiso Poetry Review: "Alto"

I.

The last pinch of salt spent with the last wick of sweat
—C. D. Wright, *"Rising, Falling, Hovering"*

SALT

I want a box with a hinged lid,
a box I can fit my whole hand into.
I want to feel my coarse temper
filtered through fingertips.
Sea. Table. Road. Rock. Kosher.
I want to overdo,
to pucker you,
to make the juices rise
from all over the stove,
drawn to over-seasoned places.
I will raise your blood pressure.
I will carry remnants
in my pockets, surprises
from the twenty pounds I broadcast
melting pockmarks across
the icy driveway. I will follow
you as I do the trucks, forgetting my way,
drawn to the rhythm of the fanning crystals
nicking bumpers, eating paint.
Take me home before we freeze.
Once inside, I will taste invisible
powder on my tongue and track
your waffled patterns across the hardwood floors.

TAIL

I wouldn't have a bushy tail,
not a fox's tail, not the kind to brush
before a party. When I picture my tail
it's hairless, waxed with jalapeño paste,
chamois buffed, and if I didn't keep it
in my pocket, it would slice the air
with all its swinging.

No wallflower tail for me.
Instead, my tail would tap a *Whisky River*
two-step inside my pocket,
insisting that I let it loose, let it go;
but if I did, I'd find it threaded
through empty belt loops
or shimmying the mike stand.

HOSPITALITY

I want no houseguests
nor in-laws living in my basement.
No out-of-luck nephews sleeping
in the spare room I use as an office.
Visitors should leave my house
before the local news comes on, even
on New Year's Eve when I might
invite a few friends for dinner,
then shoo them on
to someone else's party.

Old folks moving in
and peeing in my beds—
Not Allowed.
No moaning *Lord Lord*
or playing dominoes at the table
or pushing doors open with their walkers,
their rubber stoppers tapping
all night down these hallways.
Blind men with no sons
and no daughters will not spit
tobacco juice into coffee cans
while rocking on the front porch,
they will not splatter their dribble
on wooden floors or climb
the slow stairs to my garage apartment.

I don't want them.
When the phone rings, I won't
answer it. When friends extend
invitations, I'll decline. No crowd
at my funeral, no sympathy cards,
no flood of casseroles left at my door.

SOME QUESTIONS ABOUT A WOMAN
IN HER GARDEN

Why would a woman take off
her shoes and air her hot feet in the roses?

What kind of a woman ignores
her lover's bright call from the house,
pressing instead her cheek to the mulch,
answering the smell of grasses going to seed?

Are those clippers in her leather holster?

When she strips the velvet
from the sage and brushes her nose,
her lip, her brow with its fuzz,
does she smell the downy heads of babies?

Whose urine does she spray
on the Jupiter's Beard?

Does she love her dog,
or does she love the lavender on his coat?

Is that sweat on her lip, or mucus?

Why would a woman lie like that—
in her dark garden with her cat near the mint?

Down there in all those stiffening stems,
does she pull at the root vegetables—
the parsnips, turnips, yams?

And when she licks her rough fingers,
can you see how she aches for beets
bleeding in a bowl of Tasmanian honey?

WHEN THE MOVERS TOOK THE BED

they left the pan full of change
I kept beneath it. Emptying
my daily pockets, I put wadded bills
on the dresser and coins in the pan.
I skimmed enough quarters from the stash
to cover the cost of coffee,
maybe a sandwich. Days of plenty outweighed
days of want, and the pan grew heavy.
On moving day, nickels
sloshing like liquid on the floorboard
with the turning of each corner,
I hauled the pan to the grocer's,
shoveled handfuls of coins
into the counting machine until the pan
became lighter and my shoveling hand
dark with penny dirt. My eyes fixed on the slot
where things other than coins were spit out
as if not worth counting. All those times
on the golf course I borrowed
a ball marker, and a dozen hid there
in the pan. Aspirin, too, their crisp round edges
worn smooth against the coins. Tokens
exchanged for car washes, trips on the subway,
bags of machine-dispensed balls.
Watching the tokens pile up, I wondered
what changed my plans, why I didn't
wash the car, take the train, go
to the driving range. Pieces
from Monopoly—the thimble,
the terrier, a red hotel.
I redeemed the coins for a voucher,
the voucher for cash, then headed home,
fiddling with the green house in my pocket.

BY ANY MEANS NECESSARY

I was in such a dark mood
that when the panhandler in the hotel hallway
asked for change, I wanted to hand her
a roll of paper towels from my rented room
and tell her to roll her weakness
in a sheet and smoke it.
I can't explain this.
I want to change it.
I want to shuffle adjectives:
make it a fat hotel, a paper hallway
—a sentence, a column, a couplet.
If this fails, I wanted to tell her, braid
a string of cicada screams
into a throbbing amulet
and hang it around your neck
until I follow you, begging
for music like that. I sent her away,
then joined the circus
for a beer at the bar, the band playing
for one among the bums.

HELIUM

Packing my holster loaded with helium,
I waddled as if in a diaper, a wad
of snuff beneath my tongue. Make it two
holsters, each filled with helium,
I waddled like a duck in a diaper,
sounded like a duck when I inhaled
the helium from my leather holsters.
Six-shooters of helium, I rose above the ground
eating horehound candy and sucking
on my helium, my orals working
sucking, inhaling, candy, helium
made me cartoonish. Who eats horehound
anymore? Just something else to suck on
while I floated in my helium haze, lifted
by ballooning holsters. I'm a cowgirl
hovering above the horehound ground,
leather holsters strapped with a big buckle,
helium riding high on my hips. I love
the taste of air, draw it deep in my horehound
lungs, hold it there, floating higher, lifting
my holsters and shooting helium. I can control
my rising and my falling depending
on the helium I draw from my holsters
and hold in my huge, huge lungs. I swallow
helium deeper, then squeak it. I am a helium
holster holder hovering in a diaper holding
horehound candy in my mouth. Floating
holsters hold me. What I hold
in my holster is invisible, but it floats me.

WINKING ANN RICHARDS

Couldn't show up in a polite limo
at the capitol rotunda—
had to rumble in like laughter,
like hilarity, on your silver Harley,
your silver hair high and laughing.
My salty, sober sister,
you were still funny whisky-free,
swinging your Tom DeLay piñata.
Your winking face,
wrinkling face of Texas
charmed Molly, Willie, Lyle,
Lily, Lizzie, saluted
all their ballsy shit-kicking.

Poor George, silver foot.
We stomped our feet,
cheered your confetti-sprinkled hair.
Roll out that Baptist pallet, Birdlegs,
and tell us how the cow ate the cabbage.

BULLDOGGING, 1924

A final muscled twist of the horn and he falls,
wrestled and wrangled, bulldogged to his back.
His hooves assault the air for leverage
and flail around, defeated by a loss
of sturdy ground. A wild Wyoming wind
bellows from the snorting, slobbering nostrils
of the beaten bull while Foxy Hastings, Queen
of the Cowgirls, shakes her stringy ringlets, wet
with sweat and bull snot, and drives her boots
deep into the dirt arena, deep
into this rodeo, and, bracing herself
against convention, raises a mud-caked hand.
The weathered cowboy shifts his weight and squirms
on the fence rail, then tips his Stetson brim
in buckaroo salute. She rises, bruised
and limping, slaps the mucus from her chaps,
and Hippolyta's unfolding shadow stretches
across the ages from her jingling spurs;
the shaken bull stands and stumbles, looks
around, as if the world had lost its balance.

II.

It sings
salt sings, the skin
of the salt mines
sings
with a mouth smothered
by the earth.
—Pablo Neruda, "Ode to Salt"

ALTO

The composer whittles his quill,
fills it with opera, and writes me a note.
"Sing it," he says, but even the river

quivers at my timidity. He sees the problem,
coats the pen again, cups my chin,
then inks my mouth into a perfect oval

until my solo echoes from the hills
on an opposite shore. A river of voices
floods me, reaches for a high note, pulls it down,

and pounds it smooth against the bottom
stones, then lets it bubble up, heavier
with the weight of water. Soon, I'm orchestrating

the chorus with a stolen baton; but I hold
the low tones too long, enjoy their rumbling
in my body, annoying the composer

who blackens the oval closed
with his laden quill. I lick the sticky silence
from my lips and taste where the music was.

THE DESERT IS NOT FOR SISSIES

If I could move I would follow
the cottonwood shade. It teases the limestone
like a lover's feather. It doesn't promise

oasis. A stranger hikes alone but stops
beside me to bathe his blistered feet,
his single painted nail in the roaring springs.

I focus on his middle toe—remember it
aqua, bony. I can't look up. I lean toward
the cool water, his opened canvas bag, watch him

peel an orange, unfold it with his thumbs.
The scent tickles me, it rallies the clouds, wakes
the scorpions into flicking their tails

and dancing sideways around me. I swoon
for a dripping slice. He wipes his fingers
across the Vishnu Schist. Petroglyphs shift.

Reds, purples, yellows unravel from canyon
shadows, hiss against the scorching rocks.
If I could move, I would follow.

BRUSH ME IN

I slip on the oily trail, skin my knee
on purple, and catch myself
at the canvas edge. My boots are covered
in morning orchid. Dawn hasn't dried—
I'm following the brush, not yet kicking
up enough dust to attract attention
here in the new Grand Canyon.

Blobbing some orange on my knee
to salve it, I start again, slower.
Now, my walking sticks pierce the tacky path
left, right, pricking the weave
so a discerning eye could trace me;
but my steps make little noise,
only the suck of my boots in umber puddles.

Midday, I stop to escape the light
that wisps across the gravel and steals
the deeper hues. Thirsty, and all around me crusty,
I peel a flake of pulpy yellow, a bead of sun
dabbled on the cottonwood leaves, and chew
until it juices me. Not satisfied, I pare
another voluptuous leaf, but in its place

a drape of fingers beckons from the tree.
Stuffing my pockets with yellow
and some green, I strip the cottonwood,
release the swollen cluster clutched to a fleshy
belly. I bathe in layers of bosom,
scramble over flushed nipple, red stone.
Brush me in and camouflage me succulent.

COLORING OUR ORGASMS

We grabbed a fistful
of crayons and drew our orgasms
on the white paper covering our table.
I outlined floating sections of picket fences,
filled them with orange, yellow,
and green, pointing the tips.

You used blue to dot
a tedious line
across the table: *This could take months,*
you said, blunting your crayon,
but it's worth it. A blip in your line,
then a blue eruption, like a starburst.

Our friend's zigzagging seismographic
waves rippled then surged, surprising
us with their vigor. Pointing
to the multicolored crest, I asked,
When does this happen?
Sometimes here . . . or there, she tapped
with her red wax. *Maybe both.*
One of us gasped.

I peeled the paper skin
from the crayon and colored a field
of new grass. Behind my picket fence,
I planted an oak tree and mossed it.
In its shade, slow-eyed cows
lowered to their bellies,
awaiting your blue storm.

DEAR GERTRUDE STEIN

I've been reading Alice's *Autobiography*
and want to say that I too have hic*coughed*
and so could not take my dinner nor say my prayer,
though I think it more likely that I hicc*up*
because it shakes me. I don't know
when I will shake or when it will end,
and so I am not bored. Gertrude,
I have learned the cure for hiccups,
but I will not tell you the remedy
because it is sad to control them.
It involves water and breathing and holding
the nose, but it does not involve swimming.
It may be the housekeeper who startles you
in your Paris apartment, but here it's the lover
who frightened the hiccups from me.
That was before I knew the cure,
and that was better than using the water.
I am not bored with the lover I cannot control,
the lover who surprises the spasms from me.

GRIZZLY

The ranger glimpsed her first as she crossed the fork
in Highline Creek. He dropped his nonchalance:
"A grizzly," he whispered, "off the trail, about
a hundred yards away." I thought he might
be trying to scare us until he slung his pack
aside, abandoning his camera.

We watched for streams of light to trickle through
the pines and catch her blond hump and prove
to us her imagined poise. I held my breath.
You saw, with a shout, then leaned your head to mine,
discerning her shifting shape in the mountain shade,
distinguishing fur from fir and limb from limb—
your vision seemed enough to carry us.
I tried to spot a shift of order, a sway
of branch, a shrub shaking. I couldn't see her.

Later, we closed the tent against the night,
secured the fly, for rain, we said, then zipped
our sleeping bags together, squeezing out
unspoken hollows. Something new and wild
unmoored us. I pressed against your skin and sought
your curves and angles, finding anchor in other
familiar ways of knowing, warily
moving forward, the way the grizzly growls
before her instincts stir her on to sniff
huckleberries in the glacier wind.

FROM ALCATRAZ

I hear a woman's laughter
filter across the bay
—clear, like toasting goblets,
as close as release, unreachable.

Picture bobbing yachts lit
from within, portholes framing
New Year's Eve, silk stockings,
seams that curve then dance
to perfumed corners, touch
the satin underside of an arm.

Wave tips carry the chime
of ice in glasses until it melts,
while ripples bear the high pitches,
the bracelets' jingles, rub them bearable.

Unbearable. The call of a soiree
swing band drifts and swells,
falls back until I think it's gone,
dissolved with the voices in the bay.

Untether me. Graze the black water
with the back of your hand.

LOVE IN A POEM

it's risky to put love in a poem
like sending her out of the house
under thundering skies
walking with no umbrella
embarrassing
as if she didn't know better
than to show her nipples
like this ecstatic
in her clinging t-shirt
wet shorts announcing such
muscular thighs
rain running into love's shoes

when the sun comes out
love's still far from home
parading these public roads
with her stringy hair
love's audacity in a poem
startles motorists who swipe their wipers
then glance into rearview mirrors
to watch her leaving
wet prints on a steaming pavement

WHEN OUR BOAT HIT THE MANATEE

it was not a mediocre surprise
to any of us. It was huge.
And I wonder what the manatee
thought of our scraping his back
or his whatever with the bow
of our boat, our banged-up
rented boat with its trolling motor
churning waves in the still bay.
The manatee, or what I thought was a manatee,
heaved us from the quiet water,
then disappeared back to his nap
on the bottom of the bay.
It's not as if you need a microscope
to find a manatee, not the way you need
a microscope to find a certain-shaped cell
or to see something you cannot see with
unassisted eyes. They're not microscopic.
They're huge. So why we didn't see
the manatee asleep in the water
escapes me, even today. But what surprises
me more is that we never saw the manatee,
even when he raised the bow of our silver boat
straight out of its brackish water with a swirl
and a spray in no way mediocre. That was a show.
What never showed was the manatee himself,
just the sign of him disturbed on his lazy
morning. Then silence. Everything silent
but my screaming and cursing, my reaction
at finding myself far from shore
in a rented boat with someone so happy with surprises.

TO HAPPINESS

It's your legs that surprise me most.
Because you're a state of mind, I thought
your head might be your biggest part.
What a bombshell—helmetless,
your wild hair flying as you pedal,
sweat-plastered to your forehead.

You took that slick hill a little quickly.
And I'm not sure it was a smart idea
to ride with no hands.
I lost sight of you around the bend,
imagined finding you
sprawled on the pavement all skinned up.
I used to ride the brakes less;
now, I watch for potholes, skittish squirrels.

Nice bike. Bet it cost you.
That steel frame so retro,
the lugged joints handcrafted,
hand-painted the color of sea foam.
I want to run my hands along the tubing,
feel the spray, touch the hide,
your sweat-stained leather saddle.